FIFTY WAYS TO PRACTICE GRAMMAR

Tips for ESL/EFL Students

MAGGIE SOKOLIK

WAYZGOOSE PRESS

50 Ways to Practice Grammar: Tips for ESL/EFL Students

Second Edition

Copyright © 2018, 2023 by Wayzgoose Press

Edited by Dorothy E. Zemach. Cover design by Maggie Sokolik.

Published in the United States by Wayzgoose Press.

CONTENTS

How to Use This Book   vii

Introduction   xi

PART I
THE BIG PICTURE

1. Noticing   3
2. What's your problem?   5
3. Listen!   7
4. Parts of Speech   8
5. Grammar Police   10
6. Breaking the Rules   11

PART II
NOUNS AND VERBS

7. Action!   17
8. States   18
9. People, Places, and Things   20
10. How Many? How Much?   22
11. Nouns as Modifiers   24
12. Picture This   26
13. Phrasal Verbs   27
14. Regular and Irregular Verbs   29
15. Regular and Irregular Nouns   30
16. Problem Verbs   31
17. Then and Now   33
18. Let's Go Fishing   35
19. Make It or Do It   36
20. When I Was Young   37

PART III
ADVERBS AND ADJECTIVES

21. A Few or a Little?   41
22. Watch Closely for Adverbs   42
23. Compared to What?   43
24. You're the Best   45
25. Are You Bored or Boring?   47
26. Sing a Song of Adjectives   49
27. Acrostics   50
28. Similar to...   52
29. Comparatives in Advertising   53

PART IV
PREPOSITIONS, CONJUNCTIONS, AND
ARTICLES

30. Who's On First? (Preposition phrases)   57
31. Prepositions of Time   59
32. In, At, or On?   60
33. Articles   62
34. Conjunctions and Conjunctions...   64

PART V
SENTENCES AND THEIR PARTS

35. Types of Sentences   69
36. Actives and Passives   70
37. Relative Clauses   72
38. He Said That...   73
39. You Understand Tag Questions, Don't You?   75
40. Watch for Signs   77
41. When.... If   78
42. Do I Have To?   79
43. Twenty Questions   80
44. Mother, May I?   82
45. Environmentally-friendly   83
46. Now I'm in Trouble!   84
47. How About It?   85
48. I Would if I Could   86

PART VI
OTHER GRAMMAR TOPICS

49. The Punctuation Situation   89
50. Common Problems   90

   Bonus Tip   93

   Other Resources   95

HOW TO USE THIS BOOK

It takes many hours to become proficient at anything—a sport, a hobby, a musical instrument, or a foreign language. Many thousands of hours, in fact! For a student of English, this can seem difficult to accomplish, especially if your only opportunity to study English is in the classroom.

This book will help you learn and practice English grammar, both inside and outside the classroom. If you are already taking English classes, some of the tips will help you get more out of your classes. If you're not taking English classes – and even if you are – other tips will give you ideas to try on your own. Not every idea will work for every student. That's why there are fifty. We feel sure that many of the ideas presented here will bring you results if you try them sincerely.

Here is a suggested method for using this book:

1. Read through all of the fifty tips without stopping. Each tip should take between five and ten minutes.

2. Read through the tips again. Choose five or six that you think might work for you. Make notes about them, perhaps reflecting on why you like them. Make a plan for when you will try them, and for how long.

3. Try to choose different types of ideas: some for practicing grammatical accuracy, some for understanding new grammatical structures, some for reviewing familiar ones. Also, choose some that you can practice with a friend or language learning partner, and some that you can do alone. For your convenience, the tips are divided into two categories: **Awareness exercises,** which ask you to notice certain structures and understand how they are uses; and **Practice activities,** which allow you to put your knowledge to use. Of course, you do not have to do the exercises exactly as written. For example, if you have someone to work with, do some of the reading and writing activities as speaking activities.

4. Each time you use one of these grammatical tips, make a note about how well it worked for you and why. Remember that most of the tips will work best if you practice them several times (or even make them a habit). Don't try a tip only once and decide it's no good for you. Try the tips a few times, at least, to see how they work.

5. Every few weeks, read through the tips again, and choose some new ones. Stop using any methods that are not working for you.

The most important advice, though, is to actually *do* the suggestions you read about here. Even if you don't keep a notebook, or organize yourself in ways we suggest, find a system that works for you. If you don't do the work, you won't see the results.

Finally, try some of the other books in our *Fifty Ways to Practice* series. No one skill in English is separate from the others. Speaking, listening, reading, writing, vocabulary, and grammar are all connected. Improving in one area will almost always bring improvements to other areas too.

You can find the worksheets to use with some of the tips at: http://anglofile.com/50ways/. You are free to print and use these worksheets.

INTRODUCTION

graminaceous /ˌgræmɪˈneɪʃəs/ a
or like grass. [Latin *gramen* grass]
graminivorous /ˌgræmɪˈnɪvərəs
feeding on grass, cereals, etc.
grammar /ˈgræmə(r)/ *n.* **1** the stu
rules of a language's inflections or
means of showing the relation be
words. **2** observance or applicat
the rules of grammar (*bad gramr*

Welcome to *50 Ways to Practice Grammar*! If you've been studying grammar for a while, you might find that you are "stuck" in just a few ways of studying, or at a certain level of achievement. Even if you have just begun to study grammar, you will find a lot of ideas here to help you become better at learning.

This book will help you explore new and different ways to study and, more importantly, improve your understanding and use of English grammar.

What are some keys to learning grammar?

- Keep at it! It takes a long time to master English grammar. The good news is that you don't have to be perfect. You will get better and better if you keep practicing. Think about how musicians learn to play a song—they don't study it from a book until it's perfect. They play in order to make it better. You should do the same: practice makes perfect. (It may help to remember that native speakers of English make grammar mistakes, too—and their mistakes don't stop them from communicating in English.)
- Become aware of the grammar in the language around you. Grammar isn't just a lot of charts and examples in a book. Grammar is the way people use a language. This book will help you become aware of the grammar that exists in the "real world"— grammar on signs, in writing, in advertisements, on television, and more. Awareness of how grammar works in the real world will help you understand those charts and rules in books.

This book lists fifty tips (and one bonus tip!) for noticing, understanding, and practicing grammar. We hope that after you use and practice the tips in this book, you will think of even more on your own.

THE BIG PICTURE

How aware are you of things around you? Do you notice details, or do you not pay attention? Do you know what the phrase "the big picture" means?

Grammar awareness exercises help you to notice and focus on grammar as it is used in everyday English. As you do these awareness exercises, think about what rules or general ideas are behind what you are reading. Make notes of phrases you don't understand, or that seem different from what you know about grammar.

When we talk about "the big picture," we mean looking at grammar as a large system. We also mean thinking about your study habits, learning, and other "large" items.

❧ 1 ❧

NOTICING

As you read in English, make a habit of noticing new grammar structures. Whether you hear or read an unusual use of a verb tense, or the way that an article or preposition is used, pay attention to it. It might help also to keep a journal—either a paper one, or a file on your computer. Copy down any new or unusual grammar structures that you find in your reading. You might want to copy the sentence before or after the new structure, so you can see the grammar in context. For example, imagine you are reading and notice these sentences:

> *There are many advantages to staying home to study grammar. You don't have to find time to travel or pay for a class.*

If you didn't know that the phrase "There are advantages to..." should be followed by a gerund (that is, the *-ing* form), you could note this in your journal:

Remember: *There are advantages to X-ing things.*

Then, you could try writing some more example sentences:

There are <u>advantages to reading</u> the newspaper every day.

There are <u>advantages to working</u> early in the morning.

Remember to review your journal notes regularly to refresh your understanding.

❧ 2 ❧

WHAT'S YOUR PROBLEM?

Think about your writing or speaking in English. Write down the areas you have the most trouble with: for example, verb tenses, prepositions, articles, or using plurals correctly. After you've written them down, choose one area to focus on first. Make a plan to learn all you can about that area, and write it out as well. For example, you might read about it, make flashcards, do some exercises online, or practice by writing in a journal. Once you have focused on it for a while, move on to the next most important item on your list. Here's an example:

My main grammar problems:

1. Using the right verb tense

My plan: Read a lot of stories and underline the verb tenses.

2. Using the correct preposition

My plan: Make flashcards for common phrases with prepositions and review them every day.

❧ 3 ❧
LISTEN!

Sometimes it is easier to hear mistakes than to see them in your writing. For example, you might not see that you didn't include an article where it was needed, but you might hear the problem when you listen.

Type out a few sentences or a short story on any topic you wish. Print a copy of them on a piece of paper. Then, go to

http://naturalreaders.com

and copy and paste your writing there. Choose a voice you want to hear, and then as Natural Readers reads your text to you, listen to determine if it sounds correct. If you hear any errors, mark them on your paper, and then rewrite them.

PARTS OF SPEECH

Do you know the names for the parts of speech? Just like a professional mechanic needs to know the names of the parts in an automobile, or a doctor needs to know the parts of the body, an English learner should know the parts of speech, or grammar terms.

Make sure you know the basic ones:

- noun
- verb
- adjective
- adverb
- article
- preposition
- conjunction

There are others, which often refer to a different form of the eight basic types, or a combination of them. For example, *pronoun* is often listed as a part of speech, but a pronoun is a type of noun.

If you don't know them, use a search engine and look up "English parts of speech" and learn about any you don't know.

Write them out with examples in a notebook, or create flashcards for yourself to remember what these are.

❧ 5 ❧

GRAMMAR POLICE

People make mistakes in grammar all the time, whether it is using an apostrophe in plurals incorrectly, or using *it's* when *its* should have been used. The popularity of social media makes it easy to find grammar mistakes.

Go to a popular social media site that has comments from the public. Facebook, Twitter, or any popular blog will work. Read some posts and find as many grammar mistakes as you can. Write them in your journal, and rewrite the word, phrase, or sentence correctly.

Here's an example—what's wrong with this meme?

✿ 6 ✿

BREAKING THE RULES

Some rules in English are "intentionally" broken, for lots of different purposes or reasons.

For example, sentence fragments (sentences that are missing a subject or a verb) can be used in some situations. Normally, in writing for school or other types of formal writing, you are expected to write in full sentences. However, fragments can be effective in writing sometimes, such as in advertising, casual speech, or in a dialogue. For example, here are some ways in which fragments can be used effectively.

A. In advertising:

Ants in your kitchen? Try Ant-Be-Gone!
Everything you need for a summer picnic!

B. Political slogans might also use sentence fragments.

Maria Gonzalez. A better woman for a better city council!

C. Creative writers sometimes use sentence fragments in dialogues because they sound more natural.

"Jake, why don't you join us for coffee?"
"Sorry, can't. Meeting in ten minutes."

D. They can also be used to emphasize information:

"Wonderful! Really wonderful!"

Other rules that might be broken include:

Pronouns must agree with their nouns.

But what about, *"Each person should bring their book to class"*?

This agreement rule is usually broken to avoid the problem of designating a particular gender, or using the awkward "his or her."

Sentences can't start with a conjunction.

But, why can't they? And, who is going to stop me from doing it?

These two questions alone should tell you that there are ways to begin a sentence with a conjunction.

Sentences can't end with a preposition.

Of course they can! From "What did you write on?" to "This rule should be thrown out," prepositions are appropriate at the end of a sentence. However, don't use them if they're redundant. "Where is she at?" means the same thing as "Where is she?" The second one is preferred.

Don't split infinitives.

Splitting infinitives, putting a word between the 'to' and the verb form, has a long history. Star Trek recommended "to boldly go where no man has gone before." The poet Robert Burns "dared to nobly stem tyrannic pride." This is a rule that never made sense, and is no longer considered ungrammatical.

Try it: Look through a magazine or online article and see if you can find any rules that were broken on purpose. Write the example, and write what you think the rule should be.

❧ II ❧
NOUNS AND VERBS

Nouns and verbs are the basic building blocks of English. Nouns are described as people, places, things, or concepts. Verbs are actions or states of being.

Look at the photo of the man on the bicycle just before this paragraph. How many nouns can you name in the picture? How many verbs?

We can have sentences that are made up of only nouns and verbs:

Ming ate beans.
Noun verb noun

But we cannot have sentences that have no nouns and verbs.

The clearly big in.
article adverb adjective preposition

You should recognize that the last example makes no sense and isn't a sentence.

In this section, we'll look at the grammar of nouns and verbs, and the ways they are changed in sentences.

☙ 7 ❧

ACTION!

One type of verb are expresses action: *run, look, cook, drive.* You can usually see these types of verbs as people, animals, or things do them.

Find an article from a newspaper or online story, and locate ten different action verbs. List the ten action verbs you find, including details about how they are used.

For example: Are they used with prepositions? Are they followed by another noun (a direct object)? Are any adverbs used with them?

Here's an example, with the action verbs underlined:

> *Dolores <u>eats</u> her breakfast at eight. She <u>drinks</u> coffee every morning, too. This morning, she <u>spilled</u> her coffee on the kitchen floor.*

᪥ 8 ᪥

STATES

Other types of verbs describes "states." State verbs are those that describe what *is*, rather than what something or someone is doing. For example, *have, seem, understand*, and *know* are state verbs. It's hard to observe state verbs most of the time.

For example:

> *Dolores felt angry about her spilled coffee. She knows she can make another cup, but she is in a hurry and doesn't want to.*

In the same article as Tip #7 (or in a new article you find), locate ten different state verbs (sometimes called "stative verbs" in grammar books).

As in tip #7, pay attention to what follows the state verb: is it an adjective or a noun?

Important: Note that state verbs are not usually used in the continuous.

✺ 9 ✺

PEOPLE, PLACES, AND THINGS

For this activity, you need two pens with different colors of ink, or two highlighter pens of different colors.

Find a short story, or part of a story, to print out. One place for good free stories is gutenberg.org.

With one color, mark all the pronouns you can find. Then, for each pronoun, try to find the noun that it refers to. Mark it with a different color pen.

Notice when and where pronouns are used. Is it in the same sentence? In the next sentence? Before the noun? After the noun?

Look at this passage, for example:

> *When Louisa sprained her ankle in the game, the replaced her with Bob, a much slower player.*

The pronoun are both: the first one is a possessive pronoun (meaning Louisa's ankle; one can't really sprain someone else's ankle), and the second one refers to Louisa.

❧ 10 ❧

HOW MANY? HOW MUCH?

In English, countable nouns are ones that are able to be counted and can be made plural. "Chair" is a countable noun, and more than one chair is "chairs." We can also talk about one, two, or a thousand chairs.

"Rice" is an uncountable noun; no matter how much rice you have in a bowl, it's still called "rice."

On a sheet of paper, or on your computer, make two columns and label them *Countable Nouns* and *Noncountable Nouns*.

Look around you and list some of the things you see in the room or wherever you are sitting. Include both countable and uncountable nouns. Check a dictionary if you're not sure whether a noun is countable or uncountable. For example:

Countable Nouns: *cup, coins, camera, glove*

Uncountable Nouns: *paint (on the wall), coffee (in a cup), water (in a bottle)*

NOUNS AS MODIFIERS

We can sometimes use two nouns together so that the first one describes the second: *my jacket pocket*, *San Francisco residents*, *the car door*. In these cases, the first noun acts like an adjective, and we don't use a possessive. In other words, not *my jacket's pocket* or *the car's door*.

Noun combinations can also be used to show how one object is used or what it is made of: *a water slide, a water pitcher, a water glass, water vapor.*

Some noun combinations are so common that they are used as "compound nouns," or a single word made of two nouns – for example, *bookshelf*. Look around your room and see if you can identify any nouns as modifiers. List any you see, including any compound nouns.

For example, in my room, I see:

- a flowerpot
- a bookshelf

- a couch cover
- a table lamp
- an ash bin

Variation: Play this game with a friend. One person says a noun, and the other person tries to use it as an adjective in a meaningful way, first in a two-word expression and then a complete sentence. Take turns until one person can't think of an expression or sentence. For example:

Person A: *table*
Person B: *tablecloth*
Please wash the tablecloth after dinner.

Person B: *dessert*
Person A: *dessert menu*
I'd like to see the dessert menu, please.

PICTURE THIS

This activity focuses on using the present progressive, or -*ing* form of verbs, such as *going, walking, sleeping*.

Find an interesting photograph–it could be one of your own, one from a magazine, or whatever is available to you. You can use one of the photos in this book as well.

Write a sentence about what is happening in the photograph using the present progressive. For example: *The man is walking his dog. The sun is shining, and some children are playing nearby*.

Variation: To focus on other verb tenses or aspects, write about what happened just before the photograph was taken (past tense) or what will happen next (future aspect).

❦ 13 ❦

PHRASAL VERBS

Phrasal verbs are a combination of a verb + preposition (sometimes called a particle). This combination changes the meaning of the main verb.

For example, if someone tells you to *look up a word in the dictionary*, that is very different from *looking up at the sky*.

Some verbs have a lot of phrasal verbs associated with them. For example, related to *run* are:

- *run out* (have no more of something)
- *run over* (go over the top of something, usually with a car or bike)
- *run away* (to leave home without permission)
- *run off* (to print a number of copies)
- *run on* (to talk without ending)

Find other verbs that have a lot of phrasal forms—for example, see if you can find the phrasal verbs for *come, go, speak, bring, take,* and *give*.

Next, quiz your friends or family to see if they know the difference. (For example, you might ask them: "What is the difference between *running out* and *running over*?")

❧ 14 ❧

REGULAR AND IRREGULAR VERBS

Regular verbs do not change their spelling or form when made into a different tense, or made to agree with their subject. For example: _walk, walks, walked, walking._

Irregular verbs do change; for example: _teach, teaches,_ **taught,** and _teaching._ This may seem difficult at first, but there are irregulars that are similar to each other. The past tense of _catch_ is like the past tense of _teach: catch, catches,_ **caught,** _catching._

On index cards, or small pieces of paper, write out as many irregular verbs as you can think of (or that you can find lists of). Look at the ways that the verbs change and arrange your index cards into categories—for example, irregulars that have the _-ght_ past form (_teach-taught, catch-caught, buy-bought_).

If you remember them in groups, they will seem less irregular.

❧ 15 ❧

REGULAR AND IRREGULAR NOUNS

A regular noun is made plural by adding *-s* or *-es*; for example, *house/houses, box/boxes.*

Irregular nouns can be made plural in a variety of ways: for example, look at these pairs:

- *child/children*
- *woman/women*
- *knife/knives*
- *phenomenon/phenomena*

Find a website or grammar book that lists irregular nouns. Also, notice them in your reading.

On index or flash cards, write the singular noun on one side of the card, and the irregular plural on the back. Review and test yourself regularly.

❧ 16 ❧

PROBLEM VERBS

There are some verbs that are so irregular that they cause problems for native speakers of English as well as English learners. Here are some examples:

- *lay/lie*
- *raise/rise*
- *sit/set*
- *shine* (transitive and intransitive)

To help learn more about these verbs, create a special section in your notebook and write these verbs out with all their forms—present tense, simple past, and past participles. Also write example sentences that correctly use these words in the different forms in sentences.

Additional Note: Make sure you understand the difference between *transitive verbs* (verbs that require an object) and *intransitive verbs* (those that do not take an object). A good dictionary will indicate whether a verb is transitive or intransitive.

❧ 17 ❧

THEN AND NOW

This activity focuses on habitual activities, activities we do over and over (such as brushing our teeth), in the past and present.

Try this activity:

Take a blank piece of paper.

On one side of the paper, write "THEN" at the top.

On the back, write "NOW."

On the "now" side of the paper, make a list of things you do as a habit, such as *I see a movie every weekend*, or *I go to work at eight*, or *I do the dishes after dinner*, etc.

Now think about yourself five years ago (or longer). Write a list of things you *used to* do then, but you don't do now; for example, *I used to babysit for my niece on Saturdays*."

Now
I eat dinner with my mother every Sunday.

Then
I used to ride the bus to work every day, but now I have a motorcycle.

Notice the spelling of *used to*. The negative is *didn't use to*.

❧ 18 ❧

LET'S GO FISHING

Lots of verbs are found in the gerund, or *−ing* form after "go." For example, *I like to go <u>camping</u>.*

Think of the things you like to do. Make a list of them, using the go + *−ing* form.

Note: Not all verbs can be used like this—most that can are types of outdoor activities. So, you might like to *go surfing* but **not** *go watching TV*.

Variation: Ask your friends what outdoor activities they want to do. Use the *go + −ing* form in your questions, for example:

- *Do you want to go fishing?*
- *Do you want to go hiking?*

❧ 19 ❧

MAKE IT OR DO IT

In a notebook or on notecards, start collecting examples of when to use *make* as a main verb, and when to use *do* as a main verb.

You might write *make* examples in a different color than *do* examples, or use different color paper to help you "see" the difference.

Variation: Write another verb that could substitute for *make* or *do*. Here's an example:

The server made a lot of money last night. (made = earned)

I need to do my taxes! (do = complete)

☙ 20 ❧

WHEN I WAS YOUNG

This activity focuses on using the past tense of verbs. Go to ourtimelines.com/create_tl_2c.html and enter your name, birth year, and the current year.

This website will show you a timeline of historical events that happened during your lifetime.

Choose at least five events you found interesting and write a sentence about each of them, using the phrase *When I was...*, adding your age, and using the past tense. For example:

> *When I was five, the first DVD player was sold.*
> *When I was ten, ...*

Variation: To make this activity more challenging, use different verb tenses to describe things that happened before you were certain ages, or to talk about events after a particular age. For example:

When I was twelve, it had been three years since the space station went into orbit.

❧ III ❧
ADVERBS AND ADJECTIVES

These are the words that add information and color to your sentences. These can be single words or even phrases.

Adjectives tell us *what kind of* or *which*:

- The <u>red</u> car
- The <u>red</u> <u>sports</u> car
- The <u>red</u> <u>sports</u> car <u>behind my house</u>
- The <u>red</u> <u>sports</u> car <u>behind my house</u> <u>that I bought last week</u>

Adverbs tell us *how*, *where*, when, or *why*:

- He's walking <u>slowly</u>.
- He's walking <u>slowly</u> <u>to the store</u>.
- He's walking <u>slowly</u> <u>to the store</u> <u>to buy some vegetables</u>.
- He's walking <u>slowly</u> <u>to the store</u> <u>to buy some vegetables</u> <u>before it gets dark</u>.

❧ 21 ☙

A FEW OR A LITTLE?

When you use *few* with a countable noun, it means "almost none" (use *little* with uncountable nouns, meaning the same thing). However, if you add the article *a* in front of *few* or *little*, it changes the meaning from "almost none" to "some." Using these structures, how would you answer these questions?

- *How much money do you have in your pocket right now?*
- *How many pens or pencils are in your bag?*
- *How much free time do you have this weekend?*
- *How many email addresses do you have?*

Think of other things that you have *a few/few* of or *a little/little of.*

❧ 22 ❧

WATCH CLOSELY FOR ADVERBS

Adverbs are words that modify verbs, showing *how* the verb was done. For example, *She typed quickly.*

Watch your favorite show on television or on the Internet. As you watch, write down as many of the actions as you can from the show. Then, add an adverb describing how the action was done. For example:

Sheldon knocked loudly on Penny's door.

Variation: Did you know most prepositional phrases act as adverbs? See if you can replace the one-word adverbs in your sentences with prepositional phrases. (Don't worry about changing the meaning.) For example:

- *Sheldon knocked with his fist on Penny's door.*
- *Sheldon knocked every morning on Penny's door.*

❧ 23 ❧

COMPARED TO WHAT?

We often need to compare two objects or ideas in order to evaluate them, or make an observation about them.

Comparisons in English usually have this form:

Form: X is __-er than Y.

Example: John is taller than Carlos.

Analysis: John needs longer pants than Carlos does.

For this activity, you need to find things to compare.

Choose two similar objects from your desk, backpack, or wherever you have some small objects. For example, you could choose a short and one long pencil, or two different books.

Describe them using comparisons, and then write a sentence that explains the importance of the comparison. For example:

The yellow pencil is <u>shorter than</u> the green pencil.

Analysis: The yellow pencil has been used more than the green one.

The book by Jumpa Lahiri was <u>better than</u> the one by Hemingway.

Analysis: I recommend that you read the Lahiri book.

YOU'RE THE BEST

A superlative identifies something as being "the most" of a category of three items or more. It is usually marked with the ending *-est* or the phrase *the most*.

There are a few common words that have their own form for the comparative and superlative.

good - better - best
bad - worse - the worst
far - farther/further - farthest/furthest

For this activity, use the two objects you compared in the previous tip (#23), but add a third object to your comparison. Describe each of the items, using a superlative. Then, add an analysis or observation sentence.

For example:

The white pencil is <u>the longest</u> of the three on my desk.

MAGGIE SOKOLIK

Analysis: I never use it.

The novel by James Joyce has <u>the most difficult</u> book to read of all the books on my shelf.

Analysis: You may have trouble understanding the James Joyce book.

❧ 25 ❧

ARE YOU BORED OR BORING?

Different forms of a verb can be used as adjectives. But changing the form will change its meaning.

For example:

> *That movie **bored** me* (past tense verb).
> *It was a **boring** (adjective) movie. I felt really **bored*** (adjective) *when I saw it.*
>
> *That book interests me* (simple present verb).
> *It is an **interesting** book. I*

Notice that the meanings of *bored* and *boring* are different when they are adjectives. If a movie *bores* you, then it is a *boring* movie. (You are not the one who is boring, the movie is!)

Write sentences using the following pairs of words, being careful to indicate which was the *-ed* form and which was the *-ing* form.

1. *bored/boring*
2. *excited/exciting*
3. *interested/interesting*
4. *fascinated/fascinating*
5. *tired/tiring*
6. *charmed/charming*

Can you think of any other pairs like these?

❧ 26 ❧

SING A SONG OF ADJECTIVES

Look at a list of song titles in English. You can find these on the Internet in different ways. (For example, you can find lists of songs at http://lyrics.com). Write down any titles that have adjectives in them. Underline the adjectives you find. For example:

Happy

Dark Horse

Ordinary Love

Notice what kinds of adjectives are used with different nouns.

∾

ACROSTICS

This activity focuses on using adjectives with nouns or phrases. Write your name vertically down a page, one letter on each line. Then write an adjective that starts with the letter of each of the letters in your name. Add a noun or other phrase to modify it. Note: If you have the letter *X* in your name, use an adjective that starts with a vowel followed by *X* (such as *eXcellent*). Here is an example for a student named Maxine:

Mathematical thinker

Athletic abilities

e**X**traordinary swimmer

Intelligent person

Nice to my parents

Eager to work

❧ 28 ❧

SIMILAR TO...

Think of another person you know well. Then, write a paragraph listing the ways you are *the same* as that person, ways you are *similar to* him or her, and ways that you are *like* that person. Note the different grammatical structures used with each phrase. For example:

> *My sister and I have the same hair color. Her job is similar to mine, too. Her cat is just like mine: gray and fat!*

❧ 29 ❧

COMPARATIVES IN ADVERTISING

Look for advertisements in newspapers or magazines that use comparative forms such as *better than, newer than, the most exciting*, etc. List out the phrases you find. Practice writing an ad for something you enjoy using; use comparatives and superlatives in your advertisement.

✿ IV ✿
PREPOSITIONS, CONJUNCTIONS, AND ARTICLES

When you study grammar, it's important that you don't just read about it. Reading about something is called *passive* knowledge. It's good to know about grammar, but you want to use it, too. To do that, you need to turn your passive knowledge into *active* knowledge. To do this, you need to practice using grammar properly as much as you can. You can practice when you speak, or practice when you write.

In these practice exercises, you will use grammar in your speaking, writing, or both.

❧ 30 ❧

WHO'S ON FIRST? (PREPOSITION PHRASES)

Prepositions, like articles, are difficult because they belong more to the system of meaning than of grammar. This means there isn't a "rule" that can tell you which preposition to use, or even whether you need a preposition.

Notice prepositions and how they are used as you read. You may find that it's easiest to memorize language "chunks," or groups of words that often occur together, such as verb + preposition, or preposition + noun:

- *refer to*
- *bargain for*
- *keep up with*
- *in the morning*
- *on the outside*
- *to the left*

Keep notes in your journal of new uses of prepositions and useful expressions that you notice.

Memorizing English songs is another great way to remember prepositional phrases. Search on YouTube or Spotify for the song "Under the Boardwalk," which has many examples of prepositions of place.

❧ 31 ❧

PREPOSITIONS OF TIME

Using index cards, write the prepositions **in, on, at, during,** and **by** on separate cards.

On another set of cards, write these time phrases: **January, 2:00, March 15, the evening, 2014,** and **Tuesday.**

Draw one card from the prepositions and one from the time phrases. First, decide if they can go together. If they can, write or say a sentence using the combination. For example:

During + Tuesday = not possible

By + March 15 = *I need to make my reservations by March 15.*

When this feels easy to you, change the time phrases to: **2022, the spring, 9:15 a.m., Saturday afternoon, September,** and **midnight,** and repeat the exercise.

❧ 32 ❧

IN, AT, OR ON?

Look at a photo that has several objects in it. You can use one of your own, find one in a magazine, or go to a photo site, such as flickr.com and look at one of the photos there.

Describe the objects in it using prepositions of location, such as *in, on, by, beside,* etc. Try to describe as many locations as you can in the photograph.

1. You can also do this as a memory game with a friend:
2. Choose a picture with many objects and people in it.
3. Let your friend look at the picture carefully for one minute (or 90 seconds). Then take the picture away.

Ask your friend questions about where things are, using prepositional phrases:

- *Is there a laptop on the desk?*
- *Are there any men in the café?*
- *Are there many leaves on the trees?*

and so on. Let your friend know if they remembered correctly. Then have your friend choose a picture and give you a quiz.

❧ 33 ❧

ARTICLES

Find a video or lecture file on the Internet that has a transcript available. One good site for this is

http://ted.com

Listen to a few minutes and keep a count of the number of times you hear the word *the*. Then, check your count against the transcript. You can do the same thing for the words *a* or *an*.

Note: it can be hard to hear articles in everyday speech. Don't be discouraged if you don't hear them all.

If your native language does not have articles, this activity can help you become more aware of when *the* and *a/an* are used, even if you can't use them perfectly.

There are, of course, rules for when to use articles. You can find many sites online that explain these rules. Here is one:

https://oxfordhousebcn.com/en/how-to-use-articles-a-an-the-in-english/

But, it also helps to develop an instinct for when something feels right or wrong. To create or develop this instinct, it's helpful to read and listen to as much English as you can.

CONJUNCTIONS AND CONJUNCTIONS...

There are three kinds of conjunctions: *coordinating*, *correlative*, and *subordinating*.

- Coordinating conjunctions are words that join other words or phrases that are independent, or equal. These are: *for, and, nor, but, or, yet, so.* You can remember them by thinking of the word FANBOYS.
- Correlative conjunctions are used in pairs: *both/and, either/or, neither/nor, not only/but also*.
- Subordinating conjunctions are used at the beginning of subordinate clauses. These words include *although, after, before, because, how, if, once, since, so that, until, unless, when, while, where*, and *whether*.

Print out a story or article. Circle any of these words you find. (Be careful not to confuse prepositions such as *for* with the same word used as a conjunction.)

Study how the writer used these conjunctions. Where in the sentence (and paragraph) is the conjunction used? What kind of punctuation is used? What comes before and after the conjunction?

❧ V ❧
SENTENCES AND THEIR PARTS

Understanding how sentences are put together and how they work can make you a better writer and speaker... and even a better listener and reader!

❧ 35 ❧

TYPES OF SENTENCES

Look up the differences between *declarative*, *imperative*, and *exclamatory* statements. In your own words, describe what each means.

Get a copy of a cartoon with the words in the dialogue bubbles removed. Add the dialogue, using all three types of sentences (with the correct punctuation).

You can find printable comics of this type at

http://anglofile.com/50ways/grammar/

❧ 36 ❧

ACTIVES AND PASSIVES

Find a sentence in something you have read recently: a story, newspaper article, or magazine article. Identify the sentence as either active or passive.

If it's active, see if you can rewrite it as passive; if passive, see if you can rewrite as active (*not* all sentences can be easily – or sensibly – changed).

Write an explanation of which is the better choice, and why the writer might have chosen to write it that way. For example:

> **Active***: Irena broke the bedroom window.*
>
> **Passive***: The bedroom window was broken (by Irena).*

Explanation: If you use the passive without the 'by' phrase, you either don't know who broke the window, or you don't want to blame someone.

Note: Some word processing programs, such as Microsoft

Word, underline passive constructions when you run a grammar check, and offer a rewording of the sentence as active. However, a passive construction is *not* wrong, weak, or bad. Sometimes the active is a better choice; sometimes the passive is a better choice. Noticing passives when you read will help you develop this instinct.

Examples:

√ *I'll make dinner tonight.* (sounds best active)
X *Dinner tonight will be made by me.* (This is a strange-sounding sentence in the passive.)

√ *He was born in 1995.* (perfectly normal and good passive!)
X *Someone gave birth to him in 1995.* (a strange active.)

√ *The Great Wall of China cannot be seen from space.* (perfectly good passive)
? *People cannot see the Great Wall of China from space.* (okay as an active sentence, but more natural in the passive)

RELATIVE CLAUSES

A relative clause adds more information to a sentence.

- She is a girl.
- She is the girl in my class <u>who helped me study</u>.

Copy the beginnings of each statement below, and then complete each sentence with your own information. Some contain relative clauses already, and some will make you write your own.

- A friendly person is someone *who* ___.
- A place *where* I enjoy visiting is ___.
- I'm happy I know *how* ___.
- My best friend is someone *who* ___.
- Something *that* I need to shop for is ___.
- The month *when* the weather is nicest is ___.

Add more examples of your own using relative clauses.

❧ 38 ❧

HE SAID THAT...

When you report what someone else said, you have to make certain changes to the sentence. For example, imagine Jim says this to you: *I have to go shopping for an hour. I'll see you later.* To report what he said, you would say: *Jim said that he had to go shopping for an hour and that he would see me later.*

Do you see what changed from the original statement? Pronouns change (*I* to *he*) and verb tenses "backshift." The following three tables show how these changes occur.

present

present simple	*past simple*
"I'm a plumber."	She said she was a plumber.
present continuous	*past continuous*
"I'm eating breakfast with my roommate."	He said he was eating breakfast with his roommate.
present perfect simple	*past/perfect simple*
"I've seen that movie three times."	She said she had seen that movie three times.
present perfect continuous	*past perfect continuous*
"I've been cleaning all day."	He said he had been cleaning all day.

past

past simple	past perfect
"I read a good book."	She said he had read a good book.
past continuous	past perfect continuous
"It was snowing last night."	He said it had been snowing last night.
past perfect	past perfect
"The game had started when I got there."	She said the game had started when she got there. (*notice that only the pronoun changes*)
past perfect continuous	past perfect continuous
"I had already been studying French for two years."	He said he had already been studying French for two years. (*notice that only the pronoun changes*)

modals

will	would
"I'll visit my mother tomorrow."	He said he would visit his mother the next day. (*notice the change to the time marker*).
can	could
"I can fix my computer."	She said she could fix her computer.
must	had to or must
"All citizens must pay taxes."	He said that all citizens had to/must pay taxes.
shall	should
"What shall we do about this problem?"	She asked what we should do about this problem.
may	might
"May I leave?"	She asked if she might leave.

Look at a piece of writing in which there is a conversation. This could be from a novel or short story, for example. Rewrite the conversation using reported speech. Remember to change verbs as well as pronouns.

Variation: If you don't feel that you understand how to report speech well enough to do this exercise, look at a newspaper story and find examples of reported speech.

❧ 39 ❧

YOU UNDERSTAND TAG
QUESTIONS, DON'T YOU?

Tag questions are a way of turns a statement into a question by adding a "tag."

A question tag has two parts: a statement and a short yes/no question that asks if the first statement is true.

Examples:

- *You're going to the concert, <u>aren't you?</u>*
- *They haven't done their work yet, <u>have they?</u>*
- *She won't finish before 5:00, <u>will she?</u>*
- *I can park here, <u>can't I?</u>*

Tag questions are used mostly in spoken English. To understand how tag questions work, write out a table that looks like the example below, and fill it with at least ten different tag questions, using both positive and negative tags correctly. Use different subjects and verbs as well.

MAGGIE SOKOLIK

Tag questions table

positive statement [+]				negative tag [-]	
subject	auxiliary	verb	object	auxiliary + not	pronoun (same as subject)
You		enjoy	coffee,	don't	you?
Roger	will	attend,		won't	he?
negative statement [-]				positive tag [+]	
It	isn't	snowing,		is	it?
Laura	has never	seen	a cow,	has	she?

❧ 40 ❧

WATCH FOR SIGNS

Look at signs around you in your daily life – stop signs, warning signs, and so on.

Signs like this usually are in the *imperative* or command form. The imperative does not use *you* – it usually uses just the verb at the beginning of the command. For example:

- *Yield to pedestrians*
- *Do not touch the artwork*
- *Keep off the grass*
- *Do not enter*

Think about other signs that might be helpful around you, and write a list, using the imperative.

WHEN.... IF

Write a short story that is a series of conditionals using only *when*. For example:

> *When it snows, I can't drive. When I can't drive, I can't go to work. When I can't go to work, I don't get paid. When I don't get paid, I can't pay my bills...* and so on

Then, rewrite the story, using other connectors, such as *if, whenever*, or *every time*.

Extension: Find a copy of the children's book *If You Give a Mouse a Cookie*, by Laura Numeroff (available as a paperback, hardcover, and audio book; check an English library or an online bookseller), which is a series of related conditional sentences. After reading the book, write a similar one of your own.

❧ 42 ❧

DO I HAVE TO?

Think about your day. What do you need to do? What might happen? What shouldn't you do? Using modal verbs (*have to, must, shouldn't, don't have to,* etc.), describe your day.

For example:

> *Today, I <u>need to</u> go to the university. I <u>have to</u> catch the bus at 9:45, so I <u>should</u> get up by 8:00. I <u>don't have to</u> make coffee at home because I <u>can</u> buy some near the bus stop. Then I <u>should</u> call the hair salon and make an appointment, because I really <u>need to</u> get my hair cut. Before I go home, I <u>must</u> go to the bank to get some cash. When I get home, I <u>ought to</u>...*

TWENTY QUESTIONS

Yes/no questions have a special word order. They start with an auxiliary verb, then the subject, and then the verb. For example: *Do you know my sister?* or *Have you seen my shoes?*

Find a friend and play "20 Questions." Here are the rules.

1. All of your questions must be yes/no questions.
2. One person starts by thinking an object. To make it easier, the person can tell whether it is animal, vegetable, or mineral.
3. A second player asks a yes/no question about the object.
4. The person who has the object in mind answers only *yes* or *no*.
5. After hearing the answer, the questioner can guess what the object is.
6. The players can ask only 20 questions total (not each).

7. If the guess is correct, the winner now thinks of a new object, and the game starts over.

Tim: *I'm thinking of an object. It's an animal.*

Diane: *Does it have fur?*

Tim: *No.*

Diane: *Is it a reptile?*

Tim: *Yes.*

etc.

Variation: The person answering questions gives short answers, with the correct auxiliary verb: *No, it doesn't. / Yes, it is.*

❧ 44 ❧

MOTHER, MAY I?

When we request someone to do something, how we ask that person often depends on his or her relationship to us. We ask our brother or sister to do something very differently than if we asked our teacher or supervisor. One way to think about it is that the more "distant" that person is from us, the more words we tend to use to make a request. So, we might say to our brother: "Give me your bike!" But, to someone we knew less well, we'd be more likely to say: "If it's not a problem, could I please borrow your bike?" We also use more polite language for big requests (borrowing money, for example, instead of a pencil).

Imagine that you are in a very stuffy, hot, crowded room. You are far away from the window, which you want someone to open. Write questions showing how you would ask each of these people: (1) your sister; (2) a grandparent; (3) a classmate or work colleague; (4) your teacher or professor; (5) the President of the USA.

❦ 45 ❦

ENVIRONMENTALLY-FRIENDLY

This activity uses expressions that include *about,* for example, *to be concerned about, to care about, to do something about,* etc. Write out a conversation about the environment; for example:

A: What environmental problem are you concerned about?

B: I worry about pollution.

A: Why do you care about pollution?

B: When the air is polluted, people have a difficult time breathing. They might also develop more serious illnesses.

A: What should we do about it?

B: We need to do something about automobile emissions.

If you have a friend to work with, act out the conversation, or read it together.

❧ 46 ❧

NOW I'M IN TROUBLE!

A mixed-time conditional can be used to show the consequence of doing or not doing something in the past.

Examples:

- *I did not finish my homework, so now I don't understand this quiz.*
- *Tommy ate too many cookies, so now he feels sick.*
- *I applied for every job I could find, so now I'm working in an office.*
- *If you lost the receipt for the phone, you can't get a refund now.*

Think of events from your past that had positive or negative consequences. Write about them, using mixed-time conditionals.

HOW ABOUT IT?

Use *how about* to suggest possibilities. Use *what about* to bring up possible problems. Use either to ask a question back to someone. For example:

Alex: *I've got a week off in June. What should I do?*

Teresa: ***How about*** *spending that week at the beach?*

Charles: *Let's play golf this afternoon.*

Kathy: *But* ***what about*** *my English class?*

Julia: *How are you today?*

Franklin: *Fine, thanks.* ***How about*** *you?*

Write a dialogue in which you use these different types of questions. Read your dialogue out loud (with someone else if you have a friend to work with) to practice.

❧ 48 ❧

I WOULD IF I COULD

Imagine you could make a robot perform one daily task for you for the rest of your life. What task would you choose, and why? Use *could* and *would* in your description. For example:

- *If I could have a robot wash the dishes for me every day, I would be so happy.*
- *My robot would do all my homework for me if it could understand the instructions.*
- *If my friends could see my robot, they would want one too.*

Go to YouTube or Spotify and look for the song "El Condor Pasa," by Simon and Garfunkel. Can you understand what they are singing? If not, you can easily find the lyrics online. Learn the song and sing along! It has many nice examples of the conditional.

❧ VI ❧
OTHER GRAMMAR TOPICS

❧ 49 ❧

THE PUNCTUATION SITUATION

Strictly speaking, punctuation is not part of grammar, but it is important to good writing nonetheless, and punctuation can affect the meaning of a sentence.

Pick a punctuation mark—the comma, for example. Locate an article in a newspaper or magazine. Read the article to see where commas are placed and how they are used. Use a highlighter or a pencil and mark all the commas (or whatever punctuation mark you choose).

Try to write a rule, based on what you found. Then check your guess by looking up the rule on the Internet (see the "other resources" section in this book for some good sites). You can, of course, look up the rule first—but you will remember it better if you first try to figure it out yourself.

Practice using the punctuation mark correctly by writing a few sentences using it.

❧ 50 ❧

COMMON PROBLEMS

The secret to using the right word when using *whose/who's* and *its/it's* is to replace the apostrophe with the word *is* and then test to see if your sentence is still correct.

> ✓ *Whose jacket is this?* (correct)

> ✗ *Who's jacket is this* = <u>Who is</u> *jacket is this?* (wrong!)

> ✓ *It's my jacket.* (correct)

> ✗ *Are you it's owner?* = *Are you* <u>it is</u> *owner?* (wrong!)

Next time you write *it's* or *who's*, do that simple test.

You can use a similar test for the words *your/you're* and *their/there/they're*. Replace the apostrophe with the word *are*:

> ✓ *Is this your bike?* (correct)

> ✗ *Is this you're bike?* = Is this you are bike? (wrong!)

√ *I don't know where their house is.* (correct)

X *I don't know where they're house is.* = I don't know where they are house is. (wrong!)

√ *I think they're in the seventh grade.* = I think they are in the seventh grade. (correct)

X *I think there in the seventh grade.* (wrong)

BONUS TIP
SING IT!

Identify songs that have a specific grammar structure, and sing along. Look up the songs on YouTube.com or another site for music or videos. Look for videos that also have the lyrics, or find the lyrics separately on a website. (However, be aware that sometimes these lyrics might have mistakes in them! If you think something isn't correct, check a few different websites.)

Here are a few examples:

Conditionals: *If I Were a Boy* (Beyoncé); *If I Had a Million Dollars* (The Barenaked Ladies)

Present continuous: *Tom's Diner* (Suzanne Vega)

Future continuous: *Every Breath You Take* (The Police)

Present perfect: *Still Haven't Found What I'm Looking For* (U2)

Past/Used to: *The Way It Used To Be* (Pet Shop Boys)

Imperatives: *Happy* (Pharrell Williams)

Questions: *Dear Mr. President* (Pink)

Phrasal verbs: *I'll Never Get Over You (Getting Over Me)* (Exposé)

Mixed verb tenses: *Sound of Silence* (Simon & Garfunkel)

Gerunds and infinitives: *Can't Stand Losing You* (The Police)

Relative clauses: *The Rose* (Bette Midler)

When you sing along, you practice repeating the key grammar structures. See if you can memorize the song.

OTHER RESOURCES

Here are a few other resources that can help you with studying grammar on your own:

Websites (free)

Grammar Girl

http://www.quickanddirtytips.com/grammar-girl

"Your friendly guide to the world of grammar, punctuation, usage, and fun developments in the English language."

Grammar Monster

http://www.grammar-monster.com/

Free grammar lessons and tests.

The Purdue OWL / ESL Students

https://owl.english.purdue.edu/owl/section/5/25/

English resources focusing on writing, but including a lot of grammar information.

Books

Correct Me If I'm Wrong: Getting Your Grammar, Punctuation, and Word Usage Right! by Arlene Miller. bigwords101 publishers, 2012.

A quick guide to different problems in grammar, punctuation, and word choice.

CPSIA information can be obtained
at www.ICGtesting.com
Printed in the USA
LVHW081651220623
750522LV00030B/401

9 781938 757945